Computerised Accounting Practice Set Using MYOB AccountRight

Entry Level

This entry level computerised accounting practice set is for students who need to practice exercises of MYOB AccountRight software, students can record a month's transactions of Mobiles 4 U Limited and can create financial reports.

It covers the following topics.

- Setting Up a New Accounting System
- Suppliers, Purchases and Inventory
- Customers, Sales and Inventory
- Receipts, Payments and Expenses
- Bank Reconciliation
- Financial Reports

Syed Tirmizi
Certified Advisor

Part A
Practice Set

This page is blank.

Instructions

You have been appointed as an Accounts Assistant at Mobiles 4 U Limited, a new company dealing in smartphones. The company started trading on 1st April 2016.

You are required to create company data file in MYOB AccountRight Plus, process business transactions and produce financial reports for the month of April 2016.

Create a Company File

Company Details	
Company Name	Mobiles 4 U Limited
GST ID. Number	11-111-111
Address	45 Bay Road, Auckland, 1010, New Zealand
Financial & Payroll Year	01-Apr-16 to 31-Mar-17
Conversion Month	April
Accounts List	Start with an accounts list provided by MYOB
Industry	Retail
Supplier & Customer Layout	Item

Receive Money

1st April   Record a deposit of $25,000 cash into the business bank account as start-up capital for the business.

Spend Money

4th April   Bought a printer, computer and office stationery for $2,250 (including GST) from Office Business Supplies. Paid by Cheque number 1.

Supplier Details	
Supplier Name	Office Business Supplies
Card ID	O100
Address	23 Spring Street, Auckland, 1010, New Zealand
GST ID. Number	22-222-222
GST Code	S15
Freight GST Code	S15

Accounts Details			
Printer	$500	GST Code	S15
Computer	$1,000	GST Code	S15
Office Stationery	$750	GST Code	S15

Order an Item

5th April   Placed an order for 200 Voice V10 Smartphones at $95 each (including GST) from Speedy Communications Limited. Purchase number is 00000001.

Supplier Details	
Supplier Name	Speedy Communications Limited
Card ID	S100
Address	12 Abbott Street, Auckland, 1010, New Zealand
GST ID. Number	33-333-333
GST Code	S15
Freight GST Code	S15

Item Details		
Profile		
Item Number	V10	
Name	Voice V10 Smartphone	
I Buy This Item	✓	5-1000
I Sell This Item	✓	4-1000
I Inventory This Item	✓	1-1320
Buying Details		
Standard Cost	$95	
Buying Unit of Measure	each	
GST Code When Bought	S15	
Selling Details		
Base Selling Price	$145	
Selling Unit of Measure	each	
GST Code When Sold	S15	
Inclusive/Exclusive	✓	Prices are GST Inclusive

Receive Items

6th April   Smartphones ordered on 5th April are delivered with an invoice from the supplier. Invoice Number SC765. Purchase No. is 00000002. Convert the order into a bill.

Pay a Bill

9th April   Paid $19,000 by Cheque number 2 for the Smartphones received on 6th April.

Create a Quote

9th April   Wireless Telecommunications Limited requested a quote to purchase 100 Voice V10 Smartphones. A quote was sent for 100 Voice V10 Smartphones at $145 including GST. Invoice number 00000001.

Customer Details	
Customer Name	Wireless Telecommunications Limited
Card ID	W100
Address	41 High Street, Auckland, 1010, New Zealand
GST ID. Number	44-444-444
GST Code	S15
Freight GST Code	S15

Convert a Quote to an Invoice

11th April   Wireless Telecommunications Limited purchased 100 Voice V10 Smartphones. Convert the quote into an invoice. The invoice number is 00000002.

Sell Items

18th April   Sold further 50 Voice V10 Smartphones to Wireless Telecommunications Limited at $145 each. The invoice number is 00000003.

Receive a Customer Payment

19th April   Received a Cheque from Wireless Telecommunications Limited amount $14,500 for the settlement of the invoice number 00000002.

Create & Settle a Credit Note

23rd April   Wireless Telecommunications Limited returned 10 Voice V10 Smartphones. Issue and settle a credit note for the invoice number 00000003.

Create a Recurring Transaction

26th April   Create and record following recurring transaction for the business's electricity bill.

Supplier Details	
Supplier Name	Victoria Electricity
Card ID	V100
Address	P. O. Box 99, Auckland, 1010, New Zealand
GST ID. Number	55-555-555
GST Code	S15
Freight GST Code	S15

Transaction Details	
Amount	$200
Frequency	Monthly
Starting on	26/04/2016

Reconcile Bank Account

30th April   Prepare bank reconciliation for the month of April 2016. Company bank statement is as follows.

BANK OF RICHMOND

36 Spring Street, Auckland, 1010   **Cheque Account Statement**
TEL 18 00 NZ   30/04/2016

Mobiles 4 U Limited
45 Bay Road
Auckland
1010

Account Number
65-4321-1234567-89

Date	Details	Ref	Withdrawal	Deposits	Balance
01-Apr-16	Account opened - Initial deposit			$25,000.00	$25,000.00
05-Apr-16	CHQ 0001		$2,250.00		$22,750.00
11-Apr-16	CHQ 0002		$19,000.00		$3,750.00
19-Apr-16	Cheque deposited			$14,500.00	$18,250.00
30-Apr-16	Bank charges		$10.00		$18,240.00
	Totals		**$21,260.00**	**$39,500.00**	

Produce Financial Reports

30th April   Print or save the following reports for the month of April 2016.

     I.   Bank Register for account 1-1110
     II.   Purchases & Payables Journal
     III.   Cash Disbursements Journal
     IV.   Sales & Receivables Journal
     V.   Cash Receipts Journal
     VI.   Items Register Summary
     VII.   Item Transactions
     VIII.   Recurring Transactions List
     IX.   Bank Reconciliation Report
     X.   Profit & Loss Statement
     XI.   Trial Balance FY 2017
     XII.   Balance Sheet

Part B

Solutions

This page is blank.

Mobiles 4 U Limited
45 Bay Road
Auckland
1010
New Zealand

Bank Register

April 2016

	ID No.	Src	Date	Memo/Payee	Deposit	Withdrawal	Balance
1-1110		**Business Bank Account #1**					
	CR000001	CR	01-Apr-16	Capital introduced	$25,000.00		$25,000.00
	1	CD	04-Apr-16	Office Business Supplies		$2,250.00	$22,750.00
	2	CD	09-Apr-16	Speedy Communications		$19,000.00	$3,750.00
	CR000002	CR	19-Apr-16	Payment; Wireless Teleco	$14,500.00		$18,250.00
	3	CD	26-Apr-16	Victoria Electricity		$200.00	$18,050.00
	SC300416	CD	30-Apr-16	Bank charges		$10.00	$18,040.00
					$39,500.00	$21,460.00	

* Year-End Adjustments
Page 1 of 1

Mobiles 4 U Limited
45 Bay Road
Auckland
1010
New Zealand

Purchases & Payables Journal

01-Apr-16 To 30-Apr-16

ID No.	Account No.	Account Name	Debit	Credit Job No.
PJ 06-Apr-16		Purchase; Speedy Communications Limited		
00000002	2-1510	Trade Creditors		$19,000.00
00000002	1-1320	Inventory	$16,521.74	
00000002	2-1230	GST Paid	$2,478.26	
		Grand Total:	$19,000.00	$19,000.00

* Year-End Adjustments
Page 1 of 1

Mobiles 4 U Limited
45 Bay Road
Auckland
1010
New Zealand

Cash Disbursements Journal

01-Apr-16 To 30-Apr-16

ID No.		Account No.	Account Name	Debit	Credit	Job No.
CD	04-Apr-16		Office Business Supplies 23 Spring Street Auckland 1010 New Zealand			
1		1-1110	Business Bank Account #1		$2,250.00	
1		1-2210	Office Equipment At Cost	$434.78		
1		1-2310	Computers At Cost	$869.57		
1		6-2800	Stationery	$652.17		
1		2-1230	GST Paid	$293.48		
CD	09-Apr-16		Speedy Communications Limited 12 Abbott Street Auckland 1010 New Zealand			
2		1-1110	Business Bank Account #1		$19,000.00	
2		2-1510	Trade Creditors	$19,000.00		
CD	26-Apr-16		Victoria Electricity P. O. Box 99 Auckland 1010 New Zealand			
3		1-1110	Business Bank Account #1		$200.00	
3		6-1700	Electricity Expenses	$173.91		
3		2-1230	GST Paid	$26.09		
CD	30-Apr-16		Bank charges			
SC300416		1-1110	Business Bank Account #1		$10.00	
SC300416		6-1300	Bank Fees	$10.00		
			Grand Total:	$21,460.00	$21,460.00	

* Year-End Adjustments
Page 1 of 1

Mobiles 4 U Limited
45 Bay Road
Auckland
1010
New Zealand

Sales & Receivables Journal

01-Apr-16 To 30-Apr-16

ID No.	Account No.	Account Name	Debit	Credit Job No.
SJ **11-Apr-16**		**Sale; Wireless Telecommunications Limited**		
00000002	1-1310	Trade Debtors	$14,500.00	
00000002	4-1000	Sales Income #1		$12,608.70
00000002	2-1210	GST Collected		$1,891.30
00000002	1-1320	Inventory		$8,260.87
00000002	5-1000	Cost Of Goods Sold	$8,260.87	
SJ **18-Apr-16**		**Sale; Wireless Telecommunications Limited**		
00000003	1-1310	Trade Debtors	$7,250.00	
00000003	4-1000	Sales Income #1		$6,304.35
00000003	2-1210	GST Collected		$945.65
00000003	1-1320	Inventory		$4,130.44
00000003	5-1000	Cost Of Goods Sold	$4,130.44	
SJ **23-Apr-16**		**Sale; Wireless Telecommunications Limited**		
00000004	1-1310	Trade Debtors		$1,450.00
00000004	4-1000	Sales Income #1	$1,260.87	
00000004	2-1210	GST Collected	$189.13	
00000004	1-1320	Inventory	$826.09	
00000004	5-1000	Cost Of Goods Sold		$826.09
SJ **23-Apr-16**		**Wireless Telecommunications Limited: Credit from 00000004**		
SJ000001	1-1310	Trade Debtors	$1,450.00	
SJ000001	1-1310	Trade Debtors		$1,450.00
		Grand Total:	$37,867.40	$37,867.40

* Year-End Adjustments
Page 1 of 1

Mobiles 4 U Limited
45 Bay Road
Auckland
1010
New Zealand

Cash Receipts Journal

01-Apr-16 To 30-Apr-16

ID No.	Account No.	Account Name	Debit	Credit	Job No.
CR 01-Apr-16		**Capital introduced**			
CR000001	1-1110	Business Bank Account #1	$25,000.00		
CR000001	3-1000	Owner's/Shareholder's Capital		$25,000.00	
CR 19-Apr-16		**Payment; Wireless Telecommunications Limited**			
CR000002	1-1110	Business Bank Account #1	$14,500.00		
CR000002	1-1310	Trade Debtors		$14,500.00	
		Grand Total:	$39,500.00	$39,500.00	

* Year-End Adjustments
Page 1 of 1

Mobiles 4 U Limited
45 Bay Road
Auckland
1010
New Zealand

Items Register [Summary]

As of 30-Apr-16

Item Number	Item Name	On Hand	Current value
V10	Voice V10 Smartphone	60	$4,956.52

Page 1 of 1

Mobiles 4 U Limited
45 Bay Road
Auckland
1010
New Zealand

Item Transactions

01-Apr-16 To 30-Apr-16

ID No.	Src	Date	Memo	Debit	Credit
V10			**Voice V10 Smartphone**		
00000002	PJ	06-Apr-16	Purchase; Speedy Communica	$16,521.74	
00000002	SJ	11-Apr-16	Sale; Wireless Telecommunica		$8,260.87
00000003	SJ	18-Apr-16	Sale; Wireless Telecommunica		$4,130.44
00000004	SJ	23-Apr-16	Sale; Wireless Telecommunica	$826.09	
				$17,347.83	$12,391.31

Page 1 of 1

Mobiles 4 U Limited
45 Bay Road
Auckland
1010
New Zealand

Recurring Transaction List

Transaction Name	Type	Frequency	Last Posted	Next Due	Alerts	Remaining	Start Date
Victoria Electricity	Spend Money	Monthly		26-Apr-16	None	0	26-Apr-16

Page 1 of 1

Mobiles 4 U Limited
45 Bay Road
Auckland
1010
New Zealand

Reconciliation Report

ID No.	Date Memo/Payee	Deposit	Withdrawal

Account: 1-1110   **Business Bank Account #1**
Date Of Bank Statement: 30-Apr-16
Last Reconciled: 30-Apr-16
Last Reconciled Balance: $18,240.00

Reconciled Cheques

ID No.	Date	Memo/Payee	Deposit	Withdrawal
1	04-Apr-16	Office Business Supplies		$2,250.00
2	09-Apr-16	Speedy Communications Limited		$19,000.00
SC300416	30-Apr-16	Bank charges		$10.00
		Total:	$0.00	$21,260.00

Reconciled Deposits

ID No.	Date	Memo/Payee	Deposit	Withdrawal
CR000001	01-Apr-16	Capital introduced	$25,000.00	
CR000002	19-Apr-16	Payment; Wireless Telecommunications Limited	$14,500.00	
		Total:	$39,500.00	$0.00

Outstanding Cheques

ID No.	Date	Memo/Payee	Deposit	Withdrawal
3	26-Apr-16	Victoria Electricity		$200.00
		Total:	$0.00	$200.00

Reconciliation:		
AccountRight Balance On 30-Apr-16:		$18,040.00
Add: Outstanding Cheques:		$200.00
SubTotal:		$18,240.00
Deduct: Outstanding Deposits:		$0.00
Expected Balance On Statement:		$18,240.00

Page 1 of 1

Mobiles 4 U Limited
45 Bay Road
Auckland
1010
New Zealand

Profit & Loss Statement

April 2016

Income		
Sales Income #1	$17,652.18	
Total Income		$17,652.18
Cost Of Sales		
Cost Of Goods Sold	$11,565.22	
Total Cost Of Sales		$11,565.22
Gross Profit		$6,086.96
Expenses		
General Expenses		
Bank Fees	$10.00	
Electricity Expenses	$173.91	
Stationery	$652.17	
Total General Expenses	$836.08	
Total Expenses		$836.08
Operating Profit		$5,250.88
Total Other Income		$0.00
Total Other Expenses		$0.00
Net Profit/(Loss)		$5,250.88

This report includes Year-End Adjustments.

Page 1 of 1

Mobiles 4 U Limited

45 Bay Road
Auckland
1010
New Zealand

Trial Balance

April 2016

Account Name	Debit	Credit	YTD Debit	YTD Credit
Business Bank Account #1	$18,040.00		$18,040.00	
Trade Debtors	$5,800.00		$5,800.00	
Inventory	$4,956.52		$4,956.52	
Office Equipment At Cost	$434.78		$434.78	
Computers At Cost	$869.57		$869.57	
GST Collected		$2,647.82		$2,647.82
GST Paid	$2,797.83		$2,797.83	
Owner's/Shareholder's Capital		$25,000.00		$25,000.00
Sales Income #1		$17,652.18		$17,652.18
Cost Of Goods Sold	$11,565.22		$11,565.22	
Bank Fees	$10.00		$10.00	
Electricity Expenses	$173.91		$173.91	
Stationery	$652.17		$652.17	
Total:	$45,300.00	$45,300.00	$45,300.00	$45,300.00

This report includes Year-End Adjustments.

Page 1 of 1

Mobiles 4 U Limited
45 Bay Road
Auckland
1010
New Zealand

Balance Sheet

As of April 2016

Assets			
Current Assets			
Bank Accounts			
Business Bank Account #1	$18,040.00		
Total Bank Accounts		$18,040.00	
Other Current Assets			
Trade Debtors	$5,800.00		
Inventory	$4,956.52		
Total Other Current Assets		$10,756.52	
Total Current Assets			$28,796.52
Non-Current Assets			
Office Equipment			
Office Equipment At Cost	$434.78		
Total Office Equipment		$434.78	
Computers			
Computers At Cost	$869.57		
Total Computers		$869.57	
Total Non-Current Assets			$1,304.35
Total Assets			$30,100.87
Liabilities			
Current Liabilities			
GST Liabilities			
GST Collected	$2,647.82		
GST Paid	($2,797.83)		
Total GST Liabilities		($150.01)	
Total Current Liabilities			($150.01)
Total Liabilities			($150.01)
Net Assets			$30,250.88
Equity			
Owner's/Shareholder's Capital		$25,000.00	
Current Year Earnings		$5,250.88	
Total Equity			$30,250.88

This report includes Year-End Adjustments.

Page 1 of 1

www.ingramcontent.com/pod-product-compliance
Lightning Source LLC
Chambersburg PA
CBHW060515060326
40689CB00020B/4756